When You Grow Up : A Mother's Ode to Her Son

Devona Montgomery

illustrated by Mary Kusumkali Biswas

When You Grow Up : A Mother's Ode to Her Son

This is a work of fiction.

Library of Congress Control Number: 2023919497

Printed in the United States of America

A 2 Z Press LLC

PO Box 582

Deleon Springs, FL 32130

bestlittleonlinebookstore.com

sizemore3630@aol.com

440-241-3126

ISBN: 978-1-954191-97-6

Dedication:

I would like to dedicate this book to my two sweet boys, Jaden and Kace, and to every little boy and boy mom out there. This is for you. This is for them. This is for us.

This book belongs to :

_____

When you grow up, I hope you
know that I love you, my son.

Your heartbeat, little kicks, tumbles, and turns in my tummy, I'll never forget.

Oh, how I have loved you before we ever met.

And how I loved you more than
I could imagine after we met!

Watching you grow is so much fun.

Hearing your first words,

watching your first steps,

will always be a
sweet memory.

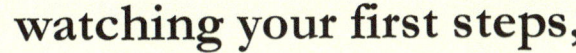

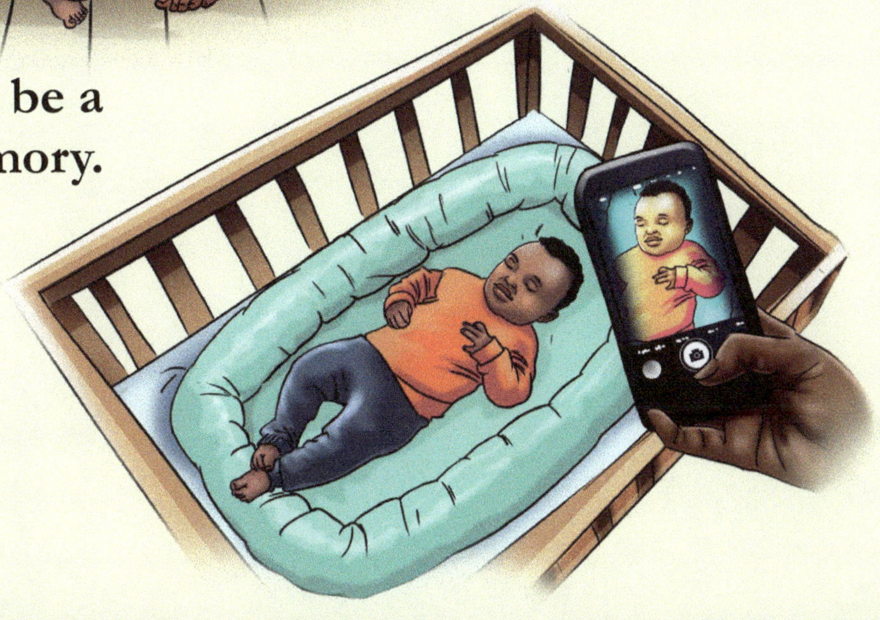

Time is moving so fast,
but you still give me kisses and cuddles,
so I won't cry today, maybe.

Your sweet laugh and smile
will always be my remedy.

But time is moving so fast,
how will we ever keep up?

I'll just enjoy the time I have with you in the meanwhile.

When you grow up, I hope you know you'll always be my baby.

I will still love you, even when you think hanging with your mom is lame.

And I'll wait all day for you to come home to me again.

When you grow up, I hope you know I enjoy every basketball, baseball, and football game.

Seeing you happy, healthy, and thriving
will forever make my heart smile.

When you grow up, I hope you remember
all the lessons I've taught you.

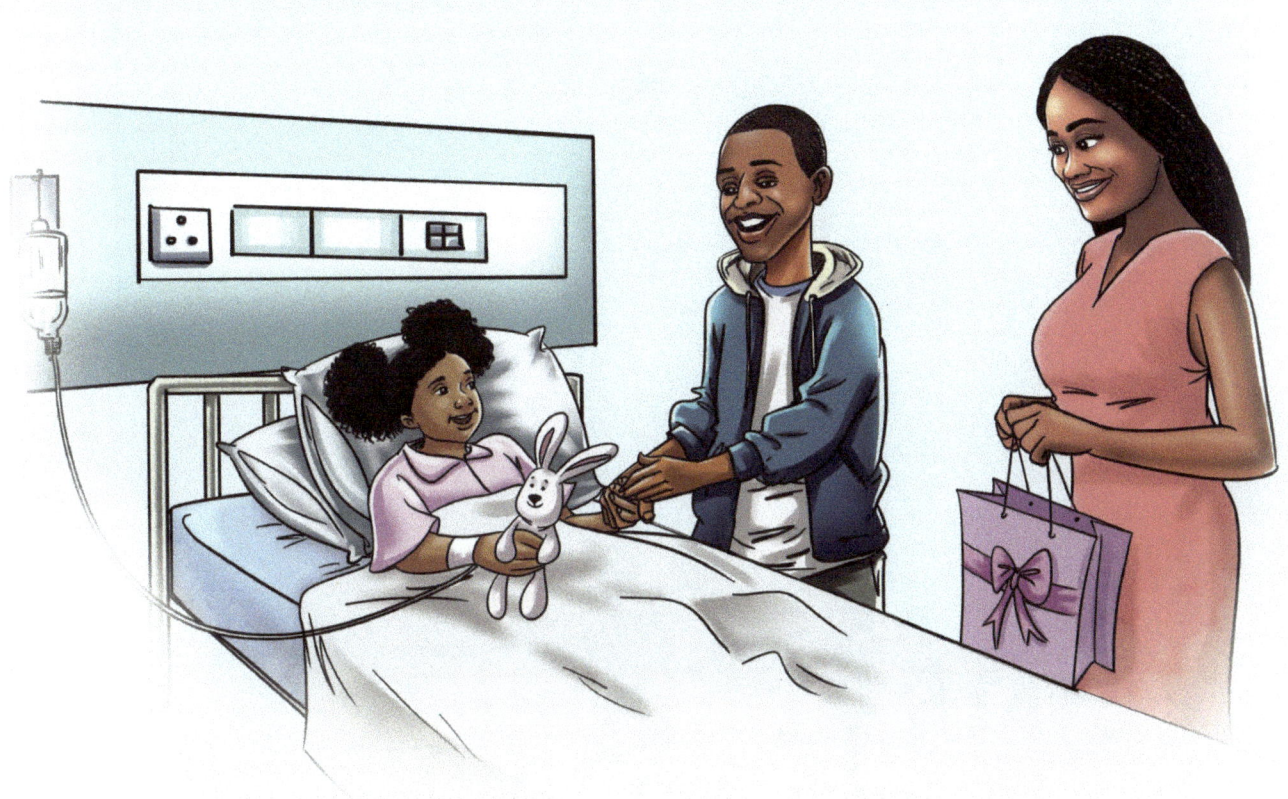

Education is important, always believe in yourself,
and kindness and courtesy can take you far in life.

To see you become the best version of yourself, there is nothing I wouldn't do.

I pray one day you'll understand
it all through your own strife.

But time keeps moving so fast, how will we ever keep up?
Now you're graduating high school,
oh where, did the time go?

And that house with the picket fence too.

At your wedding, I'll try not to sob.
And I pray that she is extra special
and made just for you.

When you grow up, I hope all your
heart's desires are filled.
Please always remember, you are
special, you are valued, and you are worthy.

And, if the time comes, I pray you are the
best father and that strong values are instilled.
My love for you knows no bounds and
will always remain sturdy.

But time has moved so fast,
we never could keep up.
Now you're all grown up. I hope you know,
I'm proud of the man,
you've become!

Devona is a native of Nesmith, South Carolina, a small rural community, located in Williamsburg County. Growing up, she always maintained the "small-town girl with big dreams" mentality. She graduated with a Bachelor of Science in Psychology from Francis Marion University and has spent most of her professional career in Human Services, Human Resources, and most recently Talent Acquisition. She always knew from the very beginning that she wanted to make a difference. Devona is passionate about healthcare, education, wellness, and creating both equity and diversity across several spectrums. This passion has led her to enter into a new realm, writing and creating. She is proud to embark on this new journey and hopes to be a contributing member to this space and community.

In her spare time, she enjoys spending time with her family and friends, traveling, and DIY projects. She is also a wife and super-mom to her two boys whom she loves dearly.

A2Z Press LLC

A2Z Press LLC
published this work.
A2Z Press LLC is a
publishing company
created by Terrie Sizemore
for the purpose
of publishing literary works by new
and aspiring writers. All content is
G-rated. We welcome your submissions
of ideas for children's literature as well
as adult and self-help topics.
Science and medicine, holidays and
other interesting topics are all welcome.
Submit queries to sizemore3630@aol.com or
PO Box 582
Deleon Springs, FL 32130

Other Books by
A 2 Z Press Authors

Spiders Love to Snuggle

There is a Poem Inside of Me

How To Succeed In College

Butterfly Beauties and Magical Moths

Beetles Boogie

Ants are fANTastic!

Fabulous Frogs and Terrific Toads

Golden Tales: Havoc in Rome

Crabs are Incredible

Just Right!

Visit our Website

Visit terriesizemorestoryteller.com or bestlittleonlinebookstore.com for our latest titles and gifts for everyone.

www.ingramcontent.com/pod-product-compliance
Lightning Source LLC
Chambersburg PA
CBHW041126120626
46547CB00019B/2879